CHOSEN

CHOSEN

Ivory Z Ward, DDS

Illustrated by Lora Look

XULON ELITE

Xulon Press
2301 Lucien Way #415
Maitland, FL 32751
407.339.4217
www.xulonpress.com

© 2022 by Ivory Z Ward, DDS

Contribution by Lora Look

All rights reserved solely by the author. The author guarantees all
contents are original and do not infringe upon the legal rights of any other
person or work. No part of this book may be reproduced in any form
without the permission of the author.

Due to the changing nature of the Internet, if there are any web
addresses, links, or URLs included in this manuscript, these may have
been altered and may no longer be accessible. The views and opinions
shared in this book belong solely to the author and do not necessarily
reflect those of the publisher. The publisher therefore disclaims
responsibility for the views or opinions expressed within the work.

Unless otherwise indicated, Scripture quotations taken from the Holy
Bible, New Living Translation (NLT). Copyright ©1996, 2004, 2007
by Tyndale House Foundation. Used by permission of Tyndale House
Publishers, Inc.

Paperback ISBN-13: 978-1-66284-394-5
Hard Cover ISBN-13: 978-1-66284-395-2
Ebook ISBN-13: 978-1-66284-396-9

Dedication

To God - Thank you for allowing me the
opportunity to reach out
to your children.

To Landon, Cayden, and Khyrin -
Dream BIG and change the WORLD!

God knew me before I was born.
It's true! He said He has CHOSEN me
and that He loves me, too.

*"I knew you before I formed you in
your mother's womb."* **Jeremiah 1:5**

I am CHOSEN to be what
God said is for me.
He has given me the choice
to be who I want to be.

8

I am CHOSEN to be a Leader. I can help the world become a better place, by helping other people, no matter their gender, culture, or race.

I am CHOSEN to be a Teacher.
I can help students learn.
Teaching math, science, and
history will be of no concern.

13

I am CHOSEN to be a Doctor.
I can help patients get better.

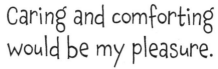

Caring and comforting
would be my pleasure.

I am CHOSEN to be a Firefighter. I can put out fires by spraying water around. I can help people out of buildings, and everyone will be safe and sound.

I am CHOSEN to be a Police Officer.
If there is a problem, call on me.
I can protect others and stop crime.
I'll be there in one, two, three!

I am CHOSEN to be a Social Worker.
I can help families when they are sad.
We will talk about hard problems, and
when we're finished, they will be glad!

I am CHOSEN to be an Architect. I can build homes for those in need. They will be sturdy and strong homes, this I guarantee.

I am CHOSEN to be a Farmer.
I can provide food for those near and far.
The food will be packaged and shipped
and arrive right where you are.

Why would you name your book Nobody Loves A Farting Princess? What does that even mean? Honestly, I have no idea. It's just something my dad used to say that stuck with me.

I was very close to my father until he was diagnosed with a stage 4 brain tumor when I was only twenty-seven. The six months I spent watching him descend from the smartest man I'd ever known, into a confused, angry zombie-man was the hardest thing I've ever been through. Even harder than anything I've endured since learning, only two years after my father gave in to his cancer, that I had the exact same type. The doctors tell me it's just lightning striking twice.

This is the story of my life, thus far.

ISBN 9781511569781

90000

9 781511 569781

Because I am CHOSEN, there are so many things that I can be. I can be them ALL through Christ who strengthens me.

To be a child of God is the
greatest blessing of all.
So make sure to listen, pray,
and answer when called.

"For I know the plans I have for you,' says the Lord." **Jeremiah 29:11**

CPSIA information can be obtained
at www.ICGtesting.com
Printed in the USA
BVRC100843050422
633410BV00001B/2